The Wilcox Quilts
IN HAWAII

By
Robert J. Schleck

Photographs by
Hugo de Vries

Grove Farm Homestead and Waioli Mission House
Kauai, Hawaii
1986

PUBLISHED BY
GROVE FARM HOMESTEAD AND WAIOLI MISSION HOUSE
P.O. BOX 1631—LIHUE, KAUAI, HAWAII 96766

Produced by Editions Limited
P.O. Box 10–G, Honolulu, Hawaii 96816

Designed by Cindy Turner

FIRST EDITION — OCTOBER 1986
SECOND EDITION — JULY 1987
First Printing / July 1987
Second Printing / September 1988
Third Printing / November 1990
Fourth Printing / August 1994

Library of Congress Cataloging-in-Publication Data

Schleck, Robert J., 1946 —
    The Wilcox quilts in Hawaii.

    1. Quilts — United States — Catalogs.   2. Wilcox
family — Art collections — Catalogs.   3. Quilts — Private
collections — Hawaii — Catalogs.   4. Grove Farm
Homestead and Waioli Mission House (Kauai County,
Hawaii) — Catalogs.   I. Grove Farm Homestead and
Waioli Mission House (Kauai County, Hawaii)   II. Title.
NK9103.W55S35   1986 746.9'7'09730730740996941 86-19482
ISBN 0-9617174-0-8

Printed in Hong Kong

The decorations used in the beginning
of this book are the patterns of quilts ULU and two unnamed
Emma Wilcox quilts in the Wilcox collection.

Cover illustration: Mahamoku Sleeping Loft, 1985.

Contents

Foreword

The Wilcox quilt collection is a carefully-tended group of Hawaiian and American quilts gathered and used by several generations of one Kauai family. Thanks to the family's gentle love of Hawaii's history, this collection has been kept in exceptional condition.

The Wilcox quilts are rich in human interest and warm relationships. The story of the quilts — in letters, notes and conversations — personalizes the objects. In the past the Wilcoxes used their quilts in their homes at Hanalei and Lihue and at their beachhouses. This museum publication offers vivid documentation of the circumstances that led to the acquisition of the quilts by the family. It also shows quiltmaking as a medium through which women express their creativity, and this history offers a glimpse of the lives of a number of early Kauai quiltmakers who were considered among the finest quilters in Hawaii.

The Board of Trustees of Grove Farm Homestead and Waioli Mission House takes this opportunity to acknowledge and thank those individuals and the Elsie H. Wilcox Foundation and the G. N. Wilcox Trust who supported the project with gifts and grants. We also express our gratitude to the members of the museum staff who so carefully prepared this book. We are grateful above all to Robert J. Schleck for making us better acquainted with the collection.

Gale Fisher Carswell
President, Board of Trustees
Waioli Corporation

Just as a quilt is made up of many pieces,
so does this story piece together one family's history
—its homes, its quilts, and the quilters.

Preface

Intended primarily as a permanent catalogue of a well-known collection of quilts, this book has come to include the stories of the family that collected them and the homes in which they were used.

This story was gleaned from letters, journals and personal notes by members of the Wilcox family. Added to these are the personal notes and publications of Ethel Damon, a family friend and historian. Since my employment by Miss Mabel Wilcox in 1971 to inventory the family collections, I have become familiar with the well-ordered sources preserved here which are the basis of this publication.

The italicized quotations threading through this story of the Wilcox quilts are taken from the *Letters of Abner and Lucy Wilcox,* a family publication by Ethel Damon, *A Record of the Descendants of Abner Wilcox and Lucy Eliza Hart Wilcox of Hawaii 1836–1950,* a family publication compiled by Elsie Hart Wilcox, and *Koamalu,* written by Ethel Damon. In addition, there are the stories of the quilters who made the quilts which were shared in 1982 as part of research for this book.

The author wishes to thank the Trustees of Waioli Corporation; Barnes Riznik, Museum Director; Mrs. Philip Palama, Secretary; the families of the quilters; and the many other friends who have made this publication possible.

Robert J. Schleck
Curator

Nu Hou, Grove Farm,
Lihue, Kauai, Hawaii
May, 1986

Waioli Mission House

Q uilts and quilting were very much a part of everyday life in nineteenth-century New England. Scraps of material were saved until there were enough to be cut and sewn into a pattern. Long hours were spent preparing a quilt to keep out the winter's cold.

It was from this rugged New England background a century and a half ago in western Connecticut that Abner Wilcox had been born the sixth child of twelve, into a family of farmer folk in Harwinton, in 1808. Even as a boy in the country school he had loved to hold church services. *"He was a great preacher,"* his niece Ellen Barker recalled. *"At recess he would get up on a big rock, and the children would listen, they never heard such sermons!"* Later, as a twenty-eight year old school teacher in the local central district school, Wilcox was filled with the spirit of the Lord and believed it was his *" . . . duty and privilege to offer myself as Missionary Teacher & c. & c. [etc. etc.] among the Heathen. . . ."*

The earlier experiences of the London Missionary Society in the South Seas taught the American Board of Commissioners for Foreign Missions in Boston to encourage its missionary candidates to be married before accepting their assignments. When mutual friends learned that Abner Wilcox must take a wife before setting out on his proposed missionary pilgrimage to the Sandwich Islands, they introduced him to Miss Hart as a prospective bride. Lucy Eliza Hart accepted Abner's proposal of marriage and at the same time offered her services

Abner Wilcox
From a daguerreotype about 1855

to be a missionary to the Sandwich Islands. "*. . . She was born at Cairo, New York, on November 17, 1814, and her girlhood was passed in Norfolk, Connecticut. While teaching school in the neighboring town of Harwinton, Lucy met Abner Wilcox.*" They were married in 1836 at the home of Deacon Norton in Norfolk and sailed from Boston, Massachusetts less than a month later on the bark "Mary Frazier" with the Eighth Company of missionaries to the Sandwich Islands.

In anticipation of setting up a new home in an unknown land, a list of necessities was sent to each mission candidate with the appointment to serve the A.B.C.F.M. Three bedquilts were listed under the category of Furniture.

Some of these possessions were also useful during the nearly four and one-half month voyage 'round the Horn' to the Sandwich Islands, as evidenced in Abner Wilcox's journal entry of December 19:

Lucy Eliza Hart Wilcox
From a daguerreotype about 1855

Monday Noon—A rainy day with a strong wind. Some of the crew are running about on deck barefoot. I have for one or two of the last nights slept comfortably under a single bed-quilt. Have sailed during the last 24 hours, 190 miles.

Abner and Lucy Wilcox arrived in Honolulu in April, 1837. Just as the word of the Lord was spread by the missionaries, so was their dress and New England way of life to change and influence the recently discovered stone-aged Hawaiian culture. *Heiau* (Hawaiian temples) and *akua* (Hawaiian gods) were replaced by Christian churches and crosses. Hawaiian thatched houses built by the enthusiastic converts to Christianity for their *kahu* (ministers) were eventually replaced by simple framed white clapboard houses cut of timber taken from the local mountains.

The two cultures proved to be curiosities for each other. The Hawaiians noticed that the missionaries used mattresses and quilts, brought with them, rather than the traditional Hawaiian mattress of layers of *lauhala* mats of woven pandanus leaves. Their cover, *kapa moe*, was a sleeping cloth made of four or five sheets of *kapa* with the top sheet being imprinted or watermarked with traditional patterns. A grey *kapa moe* and a larger brown *kapa* bedcover became a part of the Wilcox furnishings after they arrived in Hawaii. This suggests that while they were curiosities to the missionaries, they may also have been useful as additional bedding for their families. Some of the *kapa moe* show the influence of patchwork quilts.

In addition to bringing quilts with them from New England, Abner Wilcox wrote to his sister Olive about gratefully receiving boxes of donations from New England societies for their missionaries in the far away islands:

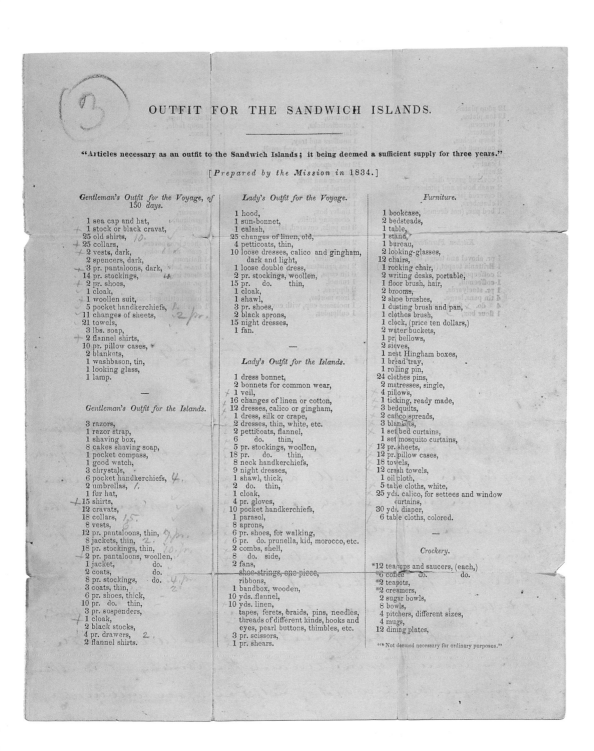

OUTFIT FOR THE SANDWICH ISLANDS.

"Articles necessary as an outfit to the Sandwich Islands; it being deemed a sufficient supply for three years."

[Prepared by the Mission in 1834.]

Gentleman's Outfit for the Voyage, of 150 days.

1 sea cap and hat,
1 stock or black cravat,
25 old shirts,
25 collars,
2 vests, dark,
2 spencers, dark,
3 pr. pantaloons, dark,
14 pr. stockings,
2 pr. shoes,
1 cloak,
1 woollen suit,
5 pocket handkerchiefs,
11 changes of sheets,
21 towels,
3 lbs. soap,
2 flannel shirts,
10 pr. pillow cases,
2 blankets,
1 washbason, tin,
1 looking glass,
1 lamp.

Gentleman's Outfit for the Islands.

3 razors,
1 razor strap,
1 shaving box,
8 cakes shaving soap,
1 pocket compass,
1 good watch,
3 chrystals,
6 pocket handkerchiefs,
2 umbrellas,
1 fur hat,
15 shirts,
12 cravats,
18 collars,
8 vests,
12 pr. pantaloons, thin,
8 jackets, thin,
18 pr. stockings, thin,
2 pr. pantaloons, woollen,
1 jacket,   do.
2 coats,   do.
8 pr. stockings, do.
3 coats, thin,
6 pr. shoes, thick,
10 pr. do. thin,
3 pr. suspenders,
1 cloak,
2 black stocks,
4 pr. drawers,
2 flannel shirts.

Lady's Outfit for the Voyage.

1 hood,
1 sun-bonnet,
1 calash,
25 changes of linen, old,
4 petticoats, thin,
10 loose dresses, calico and gingham, dark and light,
1 loose double dress,
2 pr. stockings, woollen,
15 pr. do.   thin,
1 cloak,
1 shawl,
3 pr. shoes,
2 black aprons,
15 night dresses,
1 fan.

Lady's Outfit for the Islands.

1 dress bonnet,
2 bonnets for common wear,
1 veil,
16 changes of linen or cotton,
12 dresses, calico or gingham,
1 dress, silk or crape,
2 dresses, thin, white, etc.
2 petticoats, flannel,
6   do.   thin,
5 pr. stockings, woollen,
18 pr. do.   thin,
8 neck handkerchiefs,
9 night dresses,
1 shawl, thick,
2 do. thin,
1 cloak,
4 pr. gloves,
10 pocket handkerchiefs,
1 parasol,
8 aprons,
6 pr. shoes, for walking,
6 pr. do. prunella, kid, morocco, etc.
2 combs, shell,
8   do. side,
2 fans,
shoe-strings, one piece,
ribbons,
1 bandbox, wooden,
10 yds. flannel,
10 yds. linen,
tapes, ferets, braids, pins, needles, threads of different kinds, hooks and eyes, pearl buttons, thimbles, etc.
3 pr. scissors,
1 pr. shears.

Furniture.

1 bookcase,
2 bedsteads,
1 table,
1 stand,
1 bureau,
2 looking-glasses,
12 chairs,
1 rocking chair,
2 writing desks, portable,
1 floor brush, hair,
2 brooms,
2 shoe brushes,
1 dusting brush and pan,
1 clothes brush,
1 clock, (price ten dollars,)
2 water buckets,
1 pr. bellows,
2 sieves,
1 nest Hingham boxes,
1 bread tray,
1 rolling pin,
24 clothes pins,
2 matresses, single,
4 pillows,
1 ticking, ready made,
3 bedquilts,
2 calico spreads,
3 blankets,
1 set bed curtains,
1 set mosquito curtains,
12 pr. sheets,
12 pr. pillow cases,
18 towels,
12 crash towels,
1 oil cloth,
5 table cloths, white,
25 yds. calico, for settees and window curtains,
30 yds. diaper,
6 table cloths, colored.

Crockery.

*12 teacups and saucers, (each,)
*6 coffee   do.   do.
*2 teapots,
*2 creamers,
2 sugar bowls,
8 bowls,
4 pitchers, different sizes,
4 mugs,
12 dining plates,

"* Not deemed necessary for ordinary purposes."

Hawaiian Kapa Moe
114 x 90 inches c. 1840

Hawaiian Kapa Moe
120 x 90 inches c. 1850

. . . Our boxes, one from Athol, Mass. and the other from Norfolk came safely to hand at the same time. The contents of the boxes consisted principally of bedding, such as sheets, pillow-cases and quilts. . . .

Hawaiian natives soon prized the soft cotton cloth of the missionaries and were eager to replace their sparse *kapa* with this new fabric. Cotton was growing in Hawaii but was not being made into cloth. It was being exported along with sandalwood from the dominions of Kamehameha as early as 1812. There was even an effort by the missionaries to encourage a cotton weaving industry through which the natives might increase their temporal comforts. However it proved cheaper to buy cottons than to make them. The time taken to make their native *kapa* cloth — to grow, harvest then strip the *wauke* (paper mulberry plant), pound the strips to refine and lengthen them, and finally print the bark-cloth — was soon unnecessary. Calico cotton was purchased or received from the missionaries as payment for working for them — or sometimes simply taken. Abner Wilcox often wrote to Levi Chamberlain, the missionary accountant in Honolulu, requesting that material be credited against his account. In 1841 he wrote from Hilo:

. . . You will remember we had a considerable quantity of our cloth stolen at Honolulu and out of the remainder I have paid out to natives for bringing my family from Mahukona to this place. What we have left has been mostly wet and is much spotted so as seriously to hurt the sale of it . . . I want you to send me in cloth, say one piece blue cotton; 1 piece of calico bid off at auction and sold at 14 cts. per yard (such as natives will like); half piece brown twilled cotton (I think we took ½ piece at Gen. Meeting, but on opening our boxes we have none and suppose it was stolen with other things from Mr. Bishop's house). Also we want 3 or 4 pieces of blue nankeen (narrow) such as natives use for malos. . . .

The first station the Wilcoxes were sent to was at Hilo on the island of Hawaii, where they labored until 1845. A letter from Abner Wilcox suggests that perhaps his wife was teaching sewing to the young Hawaiian girls. *"Will you please send a small box of soap, 1 salmon if large, if not large, then two, also a doz. brass thimbles suitable for girls of a doz. years of age. . . ."*

It would seem that sewing materials and implements were valued among the natives, as theft of the objects seemed to have been a complaint among the missionaries. Sara Joiner Lyman, a missionary sister in Hilo, described an incident in her letter to Lucy Wilcox at Waialua, Oahu where the Wilcoxes were transferred after Hilo:

. . . Hana has been visiting the last 2 months, so I employed Kahio's wife to do her work. She proved the greatest thief that I have ever had in my house. She stole thimbles, scissors, thread, pins, needles, buttons, wicking, calico and various other things. So now I do my work myself, i.e. making beds and sweeping. . . .

The Wilcoxes remained at Waialua, Oahu for two years and in 1846 were sent to Hanalei on Kauai where Abner Wilcox was put in charge of the Select School at Waioli Mission Station. He taught at this advanced school for Hawaiian boys for the next twenty-two years. The mission station was named for one of the *ahupuaa* (Hawaiian land division) of the Hanalei valley. It means "singing water" referring to the sound made by the many waterfalls in the nearby mountains. Abner and Lucy Wilcox arrived at Hanalei with four young sons, and over the next dozen years four more boys were born. The large young family filled the two-story frame house at Waioli, which the missionary William P. Alexander built in 1836.

Their fourth son, Albert Spencer, was born with clubfeet, and painful efforts were made in Hawaii to correct the problem, with no success. Thus in 1850 Abner Wilcox took his six-year-old son to Boston for the necessary surgery. While there, they visited family and close friends in Connecticut, causing great excitement about their missionary lives in Hawaii. Abner Wilcox wrote to Lucy from Boston:

. . . Louisa [Hart Spaulding, Lucy's sister] is quite busy with a very curious bed-quilt for you. Augusta is helping her. Made up of squares given by one and another with their names written on them. You are not forgotten, you may depend. . . .

In a later journal entry Abner again refers to the quilt:

July 25th . . . I today got a letter from Louisa. She writes that she has got our Album quilt on the frame, the one which our Sisters in Norfolk and the ladies were preparing to send you. One and another furnished a square with the name and sometimes a sentiment written in the square. Louisa I believe is taking the brunt of the work, which is too much for her, I fear. She says that some call it the most splendid thing of the kind ever made in Norfolk. . . .

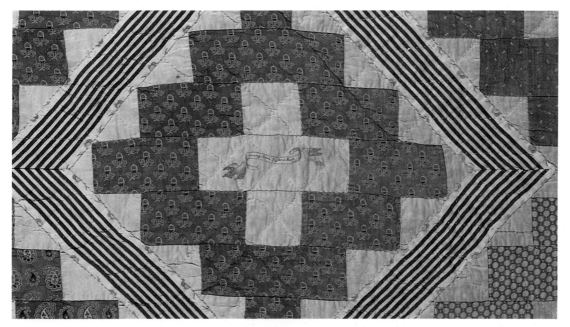

Album Quilt
Detail

Album Quilt
95 x 100 inches. 1851. Made by family and church members in Norfolk, Connecticut.

Abner Wilcox's journal entries, while in New England, tell of many visits:

Wed. Visited with Bro. Spaulding ma [family] all the forenoon. After dinner they left to return to Mr. Baker's where they expected to spend the night. They brought the 2 cheeses and a box of honey and other things, shoes, quilt & c. . . .

After the successful operation on Albert's feet, they brought the prized Album quilt back to Waioli, where Abner and Lucy Wilcox continued to teach Hawaiian children. In the early 1860's the American Board transferred the Sandwich Islands Mission to the Hawaiian Evangelical Association, and mission lands, including those at Hanalei, were divided among the remaining missionaries as part of the pensions paid them. In this way the Waioli home was deeded to Abner Wilcox.

Waioli Mission House Hanalei, Kauai. Summer, 1866.
Albert Wilcox on horseback, talking to his father Abner Wilcox.

Hart W. Corbett collection

In 1869, at the suggestion of their sons, Abner and Lucy Wilcox returned for the first time together to New England. Crossing the mainland by the new transcontinental railroad, they both contracted malarial fever and lived only a few days after reaching their old home state. They both lie buried at Colebrook, Connecticut.

Their sons kept the Waioli property, and in 1911 Albert Wilcox, who by that time was acquiring other land in the Hanalei Valley with a view to making his summer home there at the beach, bought Waioli from his brothers.

Of the American quilts that were used in the house, only the 1851 Album quilt is still in existence.

Grove Farm - Early Years

As Abner and Lucy Wilcox's generation of missionaries diminished, their sons' generation began to see the business potential of the developing islands. The Hawaiian kings sought additional revenue for their realm and the Gold Rush and Civil War on the mainland helped a variety of businesses in Hawaii to succeed.

The Wilcox sons were educated at Punahou School, founded for Protestant missionary children in Honolulu. Schooling on the mainland also encouraged these missionary boys to modify the traditional methods of the Hawaiians with Western practices. The Wilcox sons headed in a variety of directions. The eldest, Charles Hart, settled in California; Edward Payson in Connecticut; while George Norton, Albert Spencer, William Luther, Samuel Whitney and Henry Harrison remained in the Hawaiian islands, becoming important figures in economic development and in business affairs. The eighth son lived less than a year.

Years later George Wilcox reminisced with historian and friend Ethel Damon about his early years. He told her that as a boy he studied at Punahou, followed by two years of engineering at Yale's Sheffield Scientific School. Upon his return to Kauai he went to work for Judge Widemann on Grove Farm as a *luna* (supervisor) and was put in charge of surveying and laying out of a ditch planned by the Judge to encourage cane growing. George Wilcox worked about six months until the job was done, then returned to Hanalei to become a partner with his brother Albert, planting cane near their old home at Waioli. Because of

George Norton Wilcox
c. 1860

other business interests, in 1864 Judge Widemann encouraged G. N. Wilcox to lease Grove Farm plantation which he eventually purchased from the Judge.

Sophie Cracroft, an English visitor, described Grove Farm in her diary in 1861, just three years before G. N. Wilcox took a lease on the property:

. . . Mr. Widemann's Estate [Grove Farm] is beautifully situated on the edge next the sea on a fine plain or series of wavy flats, running up to the ridge of mountains. . . He has a number of small buildings (grass houses) within an enclosure bounded by a low wall of lava blocks; but the family house was a tolerably large one, with two sitting and several bedrooms, the roof open from end to end, the different rooms being merely partitioned off to a certain height by substantial wooden framework, paneled in matting . . . the house was rather old and not particularly clean. . . .

G. N. Wilcox described his new home as it was when he moved from Waioli as a young twenty-five year old bachelor:

. . . This Grove Farm house was thatched when I came here in 1864 without any ceiling, just the

Grove Farm
Lihue, Kauai, 1867

rafters overhead. The centipedes used to drop down on us and get in so much that we finally ceiled the rooms over and we never had many centipedes after that . . .

. . . Widemann's office was the little end room at the South East end of the house, that we put into the parlor afterward. Next to it was the parlor, where I am sitting now, then the dining room, then another bedroom and last a small bedroom that I turned into my office. He had a cottage where our Company cottage is. When he left, all the Hawaiians came to the auction and bid up his furniture so high that I bought only a little, barely what I needed to get along with till I could get more. Even with freight, I could get it cheaper in Honolulu. . . .

Mr. Wilcox bought a quilt titled *Nani o ka Home* (Home Beauty) on one of his trips to Honolulu. The quilt shows a contrast to traditional American quilts and the type soon became known as the 'Hawaiian Quilt'. This new quilt design was not made up of many pieces of cloth sewn together as were his parents' quilts from New England, but was made from a single, large, colored piece of cloth appliqued to a white background.

While the single piece applique quilt did not originate in Hawaii, the subject of its design — taken from nature or special events — and its original interpretation distinguish it as uniquely Hawaiian. The designer of the Hawaiian quilt pattern would usually give it a Hawaiian name that told of the inspiration for the design. Most often it was quilted in the 'echo' stitch which follows the outline of the appliqued design, giving a rippled effect.

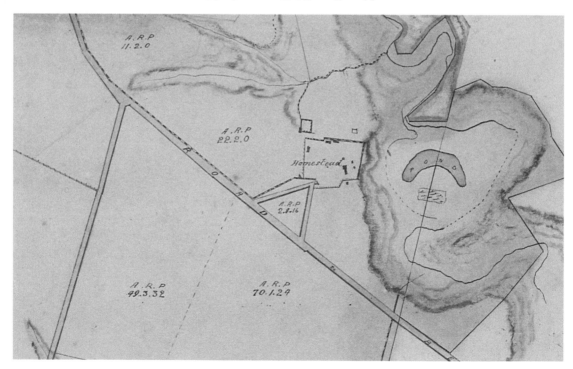

Detail of map of Grove Farm, 1873.

Nani o Ka Home
Home Beauty
75 x 79½ inches. Date unknown. Quilter unknown.

Following schooling at Punahou, another Wilcox son, Samuel Whitney, became engaged in cultivating sugar cane and served as Deputy Sheriff and in lesser governmental positions in Hanalei. In 1872 he moved to Grove Farm to manage the cattle ranching in association with his brother George. He also was Sheriff of the island of Kauai, a position he held for twenty-five years.

In 1874 Sam Wilcox married his Punahou sweetheart, Emma Washburn Lyman. She was born in 1849 at Hilo on the island of Hawaii. Emma Lyman was the youngest child of David Belden Lyman and Sarah Joiner Lyman, who arrived in Hawaii with the Fifth Company of American Missionaries.

Arriving as a young bride on Kauai, she may have brought four quilts for her new home, just as the missionaries brought quilts with them from their New England families and friends. However, Emma Lyman's quilts are single piece applique of stylized Hawaiian trees and flowers similar to the one that George Wilcox brought from Honolulu.

Samuel Whitney Wilcox
c. 1870

There is no record of when quilting in Hawaii changed from the New England patchwork designs to what is known as the Hawaiian quilt. The idea that these quilts were brought as part of Mrs. Wilcox's trousseau would suggest that the transition occurred before 1874.

Emma Wilcox remembered the name of only one of her quilts, *Ka Ulu Kukui o Lanikaula*. The other three designs were not familiar to Kauai quilters, supporting the idea that they may have been made in Hilo.

Emma Lyman Wilcox
c. 1870

Ka Ulu Kukui o Lanikaula
The Kukui Grove of Lanikaula (on Molokai)
86 x 78 inches. Date unknown. Quilter unknown.

Name Unknown
79 x 63 inches. Date unknown. Quilter unknown.
"Ulu — Breadfruit? Pink on white (old). This quilt belonged to Mrs. S. W. Wilcox and was used in the
Grove Farm Guest Cottage." EHW notes.

24

Name Unknown
76 x 74 inches. Date unknown. Quilter unknown.
"Pattern - Lilia? Pink on white. Old. This quilt belonged to Mrs. S. W. Wilcox and was used in the
Grove Farm Guest Cottage." EHW notes.

Name Unknown
Photograph of original quilt owned by Mrs. S. W. Wilcox.
"Breadfruit (Ulu)? Red on white (old). Women on Kauai in 1941 did not know the pattern. <u>Did this come from Hilo?</u> The quilt became so old and worn that we had it copied by Mrs. Lydia Waiau in 1942. The original was discarded in 1949." EHW notes.

Name Unknown
82 x 79 inches. 1942. Copied by Mrs. Lydia Ellis Waiau.
"Mrs. Waiau has asked many women for the name of this pattern. They do not know it, but think
it is <u>not</u> breadfruit. It may be a Hawaii Island pattern." EHW notes.

Grove Farm - Middle Years

S ix children were born to Sam and Emma Wilcox. They were Ralph Lyman, Lucy Etta, Elsie Hart, Charles Henry, Gaylord Parke, and Mabel Isabel. All were born at Grove Farm and received their early education there in an old guest cottage which was transformed into a school room. The Wilcoxes shared a governess with the Rice family, who lived across the valley. Emma Wilcox, who had taught in her father's school in Hilo, made sure that her children's education included more than just the basics of reading, writing and arithmetic. They all took lessons on her Chickering piano in the parlor. One learning project combined two skills: art and sewing. The children sewed through paper with brightly colored threads, following the outlines of animals drawn on the paper. A hundred years later, a wooden box full of their 'sewing projects', with their names and the dates proudly added, still sits on a shelf in the back room of the old school building, which was later called the Trunk Room.

At around that same time, 1888, Emma Wilcox finished a small patchwork autograph spread that she apparently had started in Chicago while attending the Rockford and Dearborn seminaries in 1867. Some of the calico squares are autographed by Lyman family members in Chicago and other squares include her two elder daughters' signatures, Etta and Elsie.

According to family notes Emma Wilcox's Hawaiian quilts were used on the different family beds as well as on guest cottage beds. In these same notes it appears that the Wilcox Album quilt had become a family heirloom and was stored away for safekeeping.

When Sam and Emma Wilcox's children were old enough they followed in their parents' footsteps and boarded at Punahou School in Honolulu for their formal early education. They then went on to a college education on the mainland. Ralph, Etta, Charles and Gaylord returned to Kauai, married and began their own homes. Elsie and Mabel never married and lived with their parents and uncle at Grove Farm.

Elsie, who was born in 1879, went to Wellesley College in Massachusetts after Punahou. Following graduation she returned to Grove Farm and taught in the nearby public school in Lihue for a year.

Autographed Child's Bed Cover
56 x 58½ inches. Started in 1867. Made by Emma Lyman Wilcox.

The stimulus of teaching in Sunday and public school focused her interest early on education. The twelve years following 1920 combined duties as Commissioner of Education with those as Chairman of the Kauai Board of Child Welfare. She resigned from both of these positions to serve for eight years as the first woman Senator in the Territorial Legislature.

Elsie's younger sister, Mabel was born in 1882. She was educated at Punahou, Oakland (California) High School, and Dana Hall School (Wellesley, Massachusetts), from which she graduated in 1901.

Her mother's health had always been poor and this caused Mabel Wilcox to wish to study nursing. She also felt that she might be able to improve the health of her island community. Her mother, however, hoped she would have a conventional lady's education similar to her own: music, art and poetry. Since both were equally determined, Mabel Wilcox had to agree to wait until she was twenty-five to begin nursing studies, her mother hoping she would have changed her mind or married by then.

Mabel Wilcox graduated from Johns Hopkins Hospital Training School for Nurses, Class of 1911. After

Elsie Hart Wilcox
c. 1900

some time spent in private nursing, she served from 1914 to 1917 as Territorial Board of Health Tuberculosis Nurse for the County of Kauai. During World War I she was detailed to the overseas nursing service of the American Red Cross. In recognition of this wartime service, she received two decorations: the Order of Elizabeth from the Queen of the Belgians and the bronze medal of the City of Le Havre (France) from the Mayor of that city.

By 1914 Elsie and Mabel Wilcox had encouraged their uncle to enlarge the old Grove Farm house. His practicality and sense of history shows in his choosing a design which combined his simple house with a large airy two-story Colonial Revival addition, built in 1915.

It was probably with the completion of this more formal structure that the Hawaiian quilts at Grove Farm were put in storage in the house and replaced by silk or cotton woven blanket covers and bedspreads. Annual October visits by linen salesmen made available the new bedcoverings as well as table

Mabel Isabel Wilcox
c. 1900

Grove Farm, 1985

or bed linens purchased for family Christmas gifts.

Also, there were visits by Hawaiian ladies and men with quilts for the sisters, — as gifts or for sale — possibly for money to educate a child. Hawaiian quilts continued to be used on the beds at all of the Wilcox family beach and mountain houses, though the more fragile ones began to be stored away in the new addition to the Grove Farm house.

In addition to their careers, the two sisters, who came to be known as 'Miss Elsie' and 'Miss Mabel', took over the care of their aging parents and uncle, as well as the homes and collections. Miss Mabel supervised the farm and grounds operation, supplying fresh turkeys, ducks, chickens and vegetables for the family table. Miss Elsie oversaw the housekeeping schedules at Grove Farm which were initiated by her mother. Housekeepers would arrange fresh flowers on Saturday mornings, mend clothing on Tuesday afternoons and polish silver on Wednesday afternoons. Mornings were devoted to cleaning the family rooms.

Every summer during July — the warmest and driest month — Mrs. KikunoMoriwaki, a housekeeper and laundress, would each day take out a quilt from the Korean blanket chest or the daybed in the sewing room and drape it over the second floor curved railing of the *koa* staircase in the house. It would be left out to air for the day and then would be folded and put back in its storage chest for another year. In this way the family viewed their collection of Hawaiian quilts once a year.

Peahi o Kaiulani draped over Grove Farm Koa Staircase, 1985.

Papalinahoa

J ust as the quiltmakers gave Hawaiian names to their quilt designs, island families often gave Hawaiian names to their houses. It was a fashion to use a Hawaiian decor in the simple rustic weekend houses. Dark walls and *lauhala* mats on the floors would provide a backdrop for the bright splashes of the Hawaiian quilts used on beds or on *punee* (movable couch) or *hikiee* (large Hawaiian couch with piles of pillows used for daytime lounging) in the main rooms.

Papalinahoa Beach House
Nawiliwili Bay, Kauai, c. 1920

33

In 1886, G. N. Wilcox acquired property at Nawiliwili Bay in case he should ever need to build a mill of his own for Grove Farm plantation. Landings were always made at Nawiliwili in the early days from the old schooner *Akamai*. Since there was no wharf, small boats were moored 20 to 30 feet out in the water, and natives carried passengers or kegs of sugar molasses on their shoulders to them. G. N. Wilcox built a rambling house there in 1887 and named it 'Papalinahoa' (rosy cheeks). It stood on a rugged beach, and a seawall and pier were constructed for the family's access to the water. Behind Papalinahoa were a large coconut grove and lily pond, with a waterfall created by run-off water from the canefields above.

One of Emma Wilcox's Hawaiian quilts, *Ka Pika Pua o Hale Alii* (King's Flower Vase), was used on G. N. Wilcox's bed at Papalinahoa.

Papalinahoa continued to be enjoyed by family members even as Nawiliwili Harbor was modernized and grew busier. In 1940 Elsie and Mabel Wilcox bought a quilt, *Ka Ua Loku o Hanalei*, from Mrs. Moki and Mrs. Rittmeister, two Hawaiian women of Hanapepe. The quilt, which was used at Papalinahoa, had been made and sold so that their ladies group could attend a convention in Honolulu. Since its introduction by American missionary women, quilting has traditionally been a means of church money raising. Quilting has had a primary association with the church in Hawaii since its introduction by Americans.

The sisters continued to use Papalinahoa until Elsie Wilcox's death in 1954. Two years later the house was leased to the Kauai Yacht Club as a clubhouse. It was demolished ten years later when the beach property was sold.

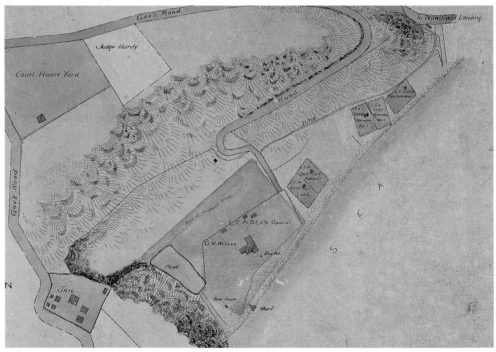

Detail of map of Papalinahoa Property, 1897

Ka Pika Pua o Hale Alii
King's Flower Vase
99 x 86 inches. Pre-1933. Bought from Kahilikalo by Emma Wilcox. Later quilted by Mrs. Waiuli.

Ka Ua Loku o Hanalei
A Distressing Rain in Hanalei
98 x 90 inches. c. 1940. Designed by Mrs. William Werner and made by a Hanapepe church ladies group.

Mahamoku

ishing to have a house in Hanalei, Elsie, Mabel, their brother Charles, their father, and their friend Ethel Damon purchased five adjoining beach front lots in Hanalei at auction in 1914.

The rustic house was planned by Miss Mabel, assisted by her brother

Mahamoku
Hanalei Bay, Kauai, 1985

Charles, and built by Sam Itchioka of Lihue. It was named 'Mahamoku' (Island of Peace). Miss Mabel later related that she shared the plans for the new house with Hart Wood, a popular island architect, asking his opinion on its design. She said he did not respond. The beach front house was placed on the property so as to have a view of Namolokama, the major Hanalei mountain, similar to the view from their grandparents' Waioli home.

. . . The house was begun in the first week of September and finished early in November, 1914. Frequent visits were made while building was going on by Sam and his children Charles, Elsie and Mabel . . . Heavy rains which washed out all minor bridges between Lihue and Hanalei at the end of September, prevented visits for 2 or 3 weeks, but ordinarily we came once and at the end twice a week. Several minor changes were made in the plans. . . .

Mahamoku Main Room, 1985

Ka Ipu Kukui o Kahului
Chandelier of Kahului
87 x 91½ inches. Date unknown. Maker unknown.
"Appliqued pink on white cotton. Bought by Mabel Wilcox from Margaret Jones, a nurse, and used as a table cover at Mahamoku. It was tattered and faded by 1941." EHW notes.

One of these changes was unexpected. Despite regular supervision, Mr. Itchioka added a three-window dormer on the ocean side of the house, much to Miss Mabel's distress.

When the house was finished, it was filled with wicker and carpenter-made pieces of furniture. Hawaiian quilts were used on all the beds, and an unquilted *Ka Ipu Kukui o Kahului* served as a table cloth on the eight-foot round pine table in the large two-story main room of Mahamoku.

Mabel Wilcox had two quilts, *Ulu* and *Ka Ulu Kukui o Lanikaula*, made to a special size by Mrs. Waiuli to fit the cots in the second floor loft at *Mahamoku*. Miss Mabel later recalled that Mr. Waiuli had told her that his wife had "worked like hell" to fit the pattern to the unusual size she had requested.

Maria Mahoe Hookano Waiuli was born in 1890 at Hanalei, Kauai. She grew up in a family of four children and learned to quilt from an aunt when she was sixteen. She married Pa'u Waiuli in 1914 just before he left to fight in World War I. When he returned, Mr. Waiuli worked for the County of Kauai on the construction of the road from Hanalei to Lihue. Prior

Mahamoku Sleeping Loft, 1985

40

Ulu
Breadfruit
92 x 64 inches. c. 1935. Made by Mrs. Maria Mahoe Hookano Waiuli.

Ka Ulu Kukui o Lanikaula
The Kukui Grove of Lanikaula (on Molokai)
91 x 64 inches. c. 1935. Made by Mrs. Maria Mahoe Hookano Waiuli.

to the 'improved road' and the use of automobiles, trips to Lihue were not made frequently due to discomfort and the length of time it took. For that reason many women did not often leave their towns or homes. However, this allowed them more time for quilting, *lauhala* weaving, feather work, shell stringing, and other Hawaiian crafts.

Mrs. M. J. 'Mama' Ouye, Mrs. Waiuli's niece, remembers going to Mahamoku with her aunt to look at the designs of the quilts she had made for Miss Mabel. When she was about age ten, 'Mama' Ouye learned quilting from Mrs. Waiuli. Since she was one of two girls in her family and there were not many other children in the area with whom she could play, much of her time was spent with the adult quilters, who eventually drew her into their projects. Her memories of those days tell a vivid story:

. . . Mrs. Waiuli, my aunt, would often get together with four or five other ladies, helping each other with their quilt projects. They would gather at table-high horses in the parlor of one of their homes, depending upon whose quilt they were working. In those days the cotton cloth was thicker, making a stronger quilt, but it also made it more difficult to manipulate the needle. The quilter would always be feeling for the needle to come through the layers of cotton plus batting, so that she could send it back —keeping a small stitch. The continuous pricking of the needle caused the fingers to become swollen and eventually callouses would develop on the fingertips, helping reduce the pain. As a result, while the women were working on a quilt project, they would find someone else to do their family laundry —which in those days was done by hand. The quilters did not want to get their hands wet because it would soften their fingertips, causing them to have to go through the misery of rebuilding the callouses.

There wasn't much talking while the ladies were quilting, as they would be concentrating on their stitches. They would make sure that they were all doing the same size stitch which resulted in a smooth, even appearance.

Maria Mahoe Hookano Waiuli
c. 1930

When a quilt was finished the quilters would celebrate with their homemade sweet potatoe wine called 'koele palau', which was made by boiling the potatoes, mashing them, adding coconut cream, and then setting it in a warm place to ferment. The juice would then be squeezed out and the celebration would begin. It might go on for a week and then the ladies would begin a new quilt.

The long-time cook at Grove Farm, Hisae Mashita, sometimes went to Mahamoku to prepare meals. She remembers that the Hawaiian quilts were often draped over the upstairs railing for airing. Elsie and Mabel Wilcox used Hawaiian quilts titled *Mokihana*, *Lilia* or sometimes *Ulu* on the first floor beds.

In 1968 Mabel Wilcox felt the quilts were being damaged by over use and brought them to Grove Farm for safe keeping.

A green and white Hawaiian quilt titled *Mokihana* was made by Lydia Kaluapiilahaina Ellis who was born in 1890 at Lihue, Kauai. She started quilting around 1919. Lydia came from a family of nineteen children and was one of five sisters who learned quilting from her mother, Elizabeth Ahiona Ellis, as well as from an aunt.

In 1920 she married Henry Wilfred Waiau, who taught Hawaiian language and was the choir leader for the Lihue Hawaiian Church. One of their four children, Mrs. Haleakala Waiau Sylvester, remembers riding with her father to Pakala and waiting while he taught Hawaiian language to members of the Robinson family, land owners on the west side of Kauai.

Mrs. Waiau quilted mostly by herself at home in the 'long room', an enclosed long hallway with many windows, next to a double parlor. Sometimes her daughter or sister-in-law would help. Whenever her sisters came calling, they would visit while sitting around the quilting horse, helping her to quilt, rather than just sitting in the parlor.

Inspiration for patterns sometimes took shape unexpectedly. Mrs. Sylvester remembers sitting with her mother on the lanai of their home and her mother saying, *"That would be nice."* The daughter asked, *"What would be nice?"* and Mrs. Waiau replied, *"That plumeria flower with a few leaves."* In that way a new quilt pattern would be created.

Mrs. Waiau was also selective about those for whom she quilted. She made quilts for Elsie and Mabel Wilcox because she held them in high esteem and knew they would prize and care for them. She taught quilting and *lauhala* weaving for the University of Hawaii Extension Service, but stopped quilting in 1948 when she began caring for her grandchildren who, according to her daughter, *"were just tall enough to run under the quilting frames."*

Lydia Kaluapiilahaina Ellis Waiau
c. 1950

44

Mahamoku Makai (beach-side) Bedroom 1985

Mahamoku Mauka (mountain-side) Bedroom 1985

Ulu
Breadfruit
81 x 74 inches. c. 1935. Made by Mrs. Maria Mahoe Hookano Waiuli.
This quilt was owned by Mabel Wilcox.

Mokihana
82 x 75 inches. Pre-1941. Made by Mrs. Lydia Waiau.
"This quilt belonged to Elsie Wilcox. A duplicate of it was given to Nell Findley, a friend." EHW notes

Lilia
Lily
80 x 79 inches. Pre-1933. Embroidered and quilted by Mrs. Haleaka Kaaihue.
This quilt was given to Mabel Wilcox as a gift.

Waioli Restored

W hile Etta, Elsie and Mabel Wilcox were at school on the mainland in the early years of this century, they saw many examples of historic building preservation. They were impressed with the historical significance of their grandparents' missionary home, Waioli, and wanted to preserve it. Their Uncle Albert felt that the house was too badly deteriorated and considered burning it down. After Albert's death in 1919, the house and adjoining mission lands were sold to Lucy Etta Wilcox Sloggett, Elsie

Senda Photo

Waioli Mission House
Hanalei, Kauai, 1927

and Mabel Wilcox. In 1921 these three sisters undertook extensive restoration of the house with a view to adding to its comfort for modern living and yet preserving its original simplicity and charm.

Once the restoration was completed, the sisters furnished Waioli with many of their grandparents' possessions that had survived the fifty year state of limbo. Their Uncle Albert had burned some pieces of furniture because of termite damage. Mabel Wilcox later told of going with her Uncle George to visit Waioli after receiving permission from his brother Albert. George wanted to go through his father's library in order to select books. While there, Mabel started to collect objects she was interested in. She put her grandmother's sewing basket in a bag and was breaking down her grandmother's small melodian to put in the bag when her Uncle George said, with a twinkle in his eye, "I don't think your Uncle Albert would approve." She explained that she simply wanted some things that belonged to her grandmother.

Ethel Damon described Waioli after the restoration:

. . . In 1921 the three daughters of Samuel Whitney, first Wilcox son born at Waioli, gathered back from the past all of the beauty and strength that could be recalled in the old homestead as well as the meeting house itself.

And the treasures now within that house! Some were there. A number have been sent back. Timepieces numbered five, much beloved of the family, and of these four are still kept safely there or in other Wilcox homes. Likewise a beautiful tapa bedspread, cherished many years by Edward Payson Wilcox, has now returned. Shells, conch and cowry, large and small, all of them much loved by Charles Hart Wilcox in his boyhood as well as in California, were later sent back to Waioli by his children.

In George Norton Wilcox's camphor chest was kept the famed album quilt which in 1921 he once more saw in his mother's room. . . .

Four other American patchwork quilts were brought to Waioli. Two were purchased in Albany, New York in 1922; a Wilcox family quilt made by Abner Wilcox's sister in Connecticut was sent to Waioli for safekeeping in 1926; and a Kentucky quilt was bought in Honolulu in 1931.

Senda Photo, 1927

Album Quilt in Abner and Lucy Wilcox's bedroom at Waioli.

Kentucky Patchwork Quilt
96 x 84 inches. Date unknown. Quilter unknown.

The Wilcox Quilts in Hawaii

Bought through Mrs. McFadden of Honolulu about 1931, the following is from a letter dated May 18, 1927 in regard to this Kentucky quilt:

We bought it from a Mrs. Gideon Miller, who is about 80 years old now. She was grand-daughter of a pioneer of Breckinridge County, Kentucky, by name of Andrew De Jarnette. He was a large land owner in his day, and the quilt was made on his place (farm, or plantation). It belonged to either the mother of Mrs. Miller or her grandmother and she told me it was almost 200 years old. I believe it was in her mother's trousseau. The flax from which the thread was made was raised on the plantation, and the cotton cloth was woven there. It was pieced and quilted there and the only part that was bought was the blue calico. Of course I have no affidavit to this, but the woman is reliable, and she had kept the quilt carefully wrapt away, as a treasure, and as quilts are usually regarded so lightly in the country, that would not have been done, had it not been unusual, —in fact I do not believe it has ever been used at all, as it is in remarkable condition. There is no question as to its age as she is, as I have said, 80 years old herself; and had older brothers and sisters and it was made on her grandfather's place. It has been a very long time too, since flax thread was used. The actual work of making thread and cotton cloth was likely done by a slave. I hope you can interest some one in it as a museum piece, as it is so typical of that period in America's history; more typical than if it were more elaborate. It would be perfect for an Early American house too; and could be used without a qualm; as it is immaculate and has never been used I am sure.

Detail of Kentucky Quilt

The Wilcox Quilts in Hawaii

The Connecticut Patchwork Quilt was well documented in Elsie Wilcox's notes:

. . . Green and tan patchwork quilt. Made by Olive Catlin, sister of Abner Wilcox. Green material was from Lois Wilcox's dress. Lois was the wife of Aaron Wilcox and mother of Abner. Yellow material is French Calico, $1.00 per yard, from a dress of Elvira, first wife of Charles Wilcox, Abner's brother. This quilt was owned by Ellen Welton (Catlin) Barker, daughter of Maria Wilcox Welton, who was also a sister of Abner. Ellen's mother, Maria, died while Ellen was young and she was brought up by her aunt, Olive Catlin. She married Virgil Barker and they moved to California, living in Redlands and later in Los Angeles. She gave this quilt to Charles Hart Wilcox (son of Charles Hart Wilcox and grandson of Abner) of Piedmont, California and he gave it to Waioli Mission House in 1926. . . . (EHW notes)

Ellen Barker remembered Olive Catlin's work:

No one was ever idle in that old farmhouse at Harwinton. That's how my mother Olive knew how to card and spin so well . . . Mother Olive wove beautiful blankets of wool with some white linen yarn and dark blue wool in squares. She made patchwork quilts too!

The refurnishing of the Waioli Mission House was one of the earliest historic house restorations in Hawaii. The sisters looked forward to days spent at Waioli and while there would show people through their grandparents' home. If the granddaughters were not staying there, people who wandered back through the Waioli gates would find the doors to the house unlocked and could show themselves through the preserved Mission House.

Waioli Mission House was incorporated as a museum in 1953, and an endowment was set up by the sisters to insure its preservation.

Waioli Mission House
Hanalei, Kauai, 1985

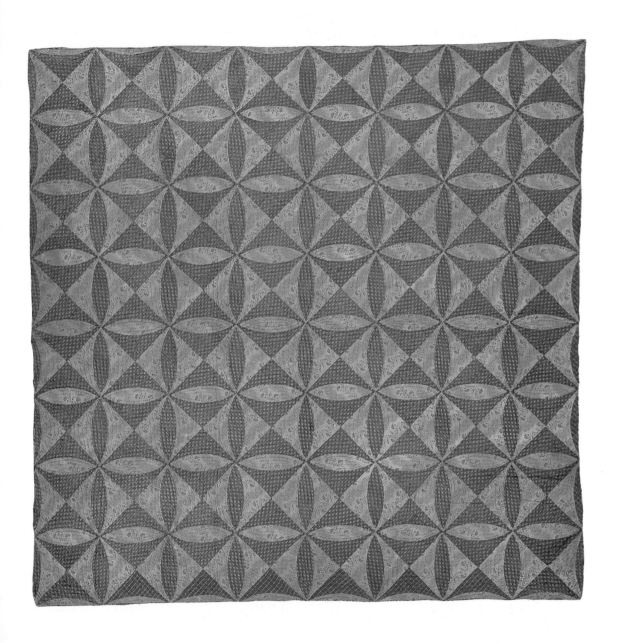

Connecticut Patchwork Quilt
84 x 87 inches. c. 1850. Quilt made by Olive Catlin, sister of Abner Wilcox.

American Patchwork Quilt
68 x 82½ inches. Date unknown. Quilter unknown.
Bought in Albany by Elsie H. Wilcox in 1922.

American Patchwork Quilt
68½ x 82½ inches. Date unknown. Quilter unknown.
Bought in Albany by Elsie H. Wilcox in 1922.

Unquilted Patchwork Spread
75 x 80 inches. Date unknown. Quilter unknown.
This pink and white spread was kept at the Grove Farm house for many years, and is now at Waioli Mission House.

Patchwork Quilt
69 x 76 inches. 1955. Made by Helen Lyman.

Mokihana Club Exhibition

On March 1, 1933, the Mokihana Club, a Kauai women's literary, civic and social club, drew attention to Hawaiian quilt-making when it gathered together an extensive exhibition of 108 quilts at the Lihue Parish Hall. Emma, Elsie and Mabel Wilcox were among the club's founders in 1905 and they lent eleven of the Wilcox family quilts for the exhibit, the first of its kind on the island. George Wilcox's

Senda Photo, 1933

Mokihana Club 1933 Exhibit. Lihue Parish Hall.
The Hawaiian Crown and Coat-of-Arms quilt on the front left apron of the stage is the quilt given to Mabel Wilcox by Mrs. Kupihea.

Hawaiian Crown and Coat-of-Arms
82 x 77 inches. Pre-1933. Made by Mrs. Kupihea.
Mr. and Mrs. Kupihea lived at Anahola and owned land at Waipa, which Mabel Wilcox bought from them. At the time of the sale Mrs. Kupihea gave Miss Mabel this quilt. Later Miss Mabel gave the Waipa land to Waioli Mission, but the quilt has always been kept at Grove Farm.

quilt, Emma Wilcox's early Hilo quilts and six quilts collected by Elsie and Mabel Wilcox were part of the impressive display.

A number of expert Kauai quiltmakers took part in the Mokihana Club exhibition. There they discussed their designs and techniques which were considered to be individual. Any attempt to copy either without the permission of the originator was frowned upon. One of the exhibit organizers, Edith Rice Plews, gave a talk to the club members in which she commented on the quilting techniques of an island quilter, Mrs. Hughes Montgomery:

Mrs. Montgomery can sew very fast and still make her stitches small and even; she "follows the pattern" freehand. I want you to notice how cleverly she conceals the knot in the stuffing of the quilt. She wears a thimble on the middle finger of her right hand, but no shield or glove finger on her left, as she must feel the needle.

Kalei Lois Kapule was born at Kilauea in 1884. She married Hughes Kalei Montgomery, who was the jailer for Kauai. They first lived in a house by the old jail above Nawiliwili, on the present site of the Bulk Sugar Storage Plant. The Montgomerys then moved to a house by the 'new jail' at Wailua in 1936, when it had just been completed. The jail became known locally as 'Montgomery Hotel' and was demolished in 1978 to make way for a new correctional center.

Kalei Lois Kapule Montgomery
1933

The Montgomerys had a family of eighteen children. Mrs. Montgomery is thought to have learned quilting when she was about 30 years old from her aunt, Louisa Kaiwi. She quilted by herself during the daylight hours, sitting on her parlor floor, working at low quilting horses. According to her daughters, Mrs. Esther Telles and Mrs. Jennie Kimble, "*. . . quilting needed an angled light, early morning or late afternoon. She would not quilt at high noon because the needle would just keep poking, and it hurt.*"

Mrs. Montgomery gave most of her quilts to her children, family and friends. She would only take orders for quilts from a few other people.

Many of Mrs. Waiau and Mrs. Wailui's quilts were also included as part of the Wilcox collection at the 1933 exhibition.

Mokihana Club 1933 Exhibit
The quilt in the center is Emma Wilcox's Ka Pika Pua o Hale Alii.

Mokihana Club 1933 Exhibit
Left to right at the quilting horses: Adelaide Gifford carding wool, Mrs. Milia Kaiawe,
Mrs. Leialoha Kanoho, Mrs. Akao Lock, Mrs. Louisa Malina, and Mrs. Kalei Montgomery quilting.

Hawaiian Flag and Coat-of-Arms
74 x 61 inches. c. 1940. Made by Mrs. Kalei Lois Kapule Montgomery.
Several years after the Mokihana Club Exhibit Mabel Wilcox bought this quilt at a Salvation Army Fair.

Ulu
Breadfruit.
83 x 81 inches. Pre-1933. Quilter unknown.
This quilt was owned by Elsie Wilcox and was kept at Grove Farm.

Lilia o Na Kalo
Calla Lily.
82 x 80 inches. Pre-1933. Made by Mrs. Maria Pihaleo Ellis.
This quilt was given to Elsie Wilcox, and was kept at the Grove Farm house.

Lilia Hoku
Star Lily.
78 x 76 inches. Pre-1933. Made by Mrs. Lydia Ellis Waiau.
This quilt belonged to Elsie Wilcox and was kept at Grove Farm.

Ulu
Breadfruit
79 x 68 inches. Pre-1933. Made by Mrs. Maria Mahoe Hookano Waiuli.
"Mabel Wilcox bought this quilt as a gift for Margaret Bergen. Miss Mabel became interested in social service work under Miss Bergen in Honolulu in 1911. After Miss Bergen's death, the quilt was returned to Miss Mabel and is now a part of the collection at the Grove Farm house. Mrs. Waiuli also made this same pattern in pink and white for Elsie Wilcox, who gave it to Louise Mitchell in 1940." EHW notes.

Ka Ipu Kukui o Kahului
Chandelier of Kahului
88 x 79 inches. Pre-1933. Made by Mrs. Maria Mahoe Hookano Waiuli.
This quilt was copied from an unquilted pink on white used as a table cover at Mahamoku.
When it became worn, Mrs. Waiuli made this quilted copy.

Grove Farm - Later Years

S am Wilcox died at Grove Farm in 1929 at the age of 81. G. N. Wilcox was 93 years old when he died in 1933 in Honolulu. He left his plantation to all of his nieces and nephews equally, as well as lifetime use of his plantation home at Grove Farm and Papalinahoa to Miss Elsie and Miss Mabel. Emma Wilcox died at Grove Farm in 1934.

The two sisters acquired from their parents, uncle and grandparents a deep sense of history and continued to research and add to the collections begun by their family. Just as G. N.

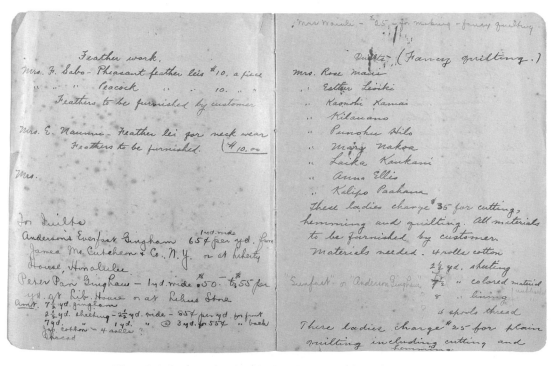

Elsie Wilcox's notebook of Hawaiian Arts and Crafts. c. 1920

Pua Geranium

Geranium Flower

82 x 78 inches. Date unknown. Quilter unknown.
This quilt belonged to Elsie Wilcox and was kept at Grove Farm.

Wilcox thought of himself as a 'steward of the land', his nieces became the caretakers of all that had been gathered by three generations of their family in Hawaii. They continued to collect objects, both past and present, which demonstrated the history and art of their island home.

Miss Elsie's involvement with the Hawaiian arts and crafts being made on Kauai shows in one of her notebooks in which she listed *lauhala* weavers, featherworkers, quilters and needleworkers. As early as the 1920's Miss Elsie, as a member of the Kauai Board of the YWCA, brought together quilters and interested buyers. Family and friends on Oahu and Molokai contacted her with patterns and colors they would like to have made into a quilt for themselves. Because of her association with Hawaiian ladies in the community, Miss Elsie was able to arrange for quilts to be made, which provided a small commission for the YWCA, extra income for the quilter, and encouraged the continuance of quilting.

In the 1920's the average cost of a quilt was twenty-five dollars plus the cost of the material. By the 1930's the quilting cost had risen to thirty-five dollars. World War II created hardships for this arrangement when buyers frequently had to supply the materials because of the shortage of goods in island stores.

Another Kauai quilter represented in the collection was Lahapa Kamakalii Opiopio who was born in 1880 at Anahola, Kauai. She learned to quilt as a student at the Kamehameha School for Girls in Honolulu. After she graduated in 1903, she returned to Kauai and married Lawrence James Mundon of Kapaa in 1905. They had seven children and adopted one child. After Mr. Mundon died in 1918, she married Solomon Opio.

When Mrs. Opio moved to Kapaa, she was one of only three women who quilted there. She quilted alone in her parlor, sitting on a *lauhala* mat while working at her low quilt horses. She always used wool batting in her quilts, rather than cotton, because the wool would hold together better during laundering and not lump.

Three of her daughters would help to applique the pattern before Mrs. Opio did the quilting. If they did not do it correctly, they would have to rip out their stitches and do it over. The youngest daughter had to get up early to sweep and mop the floor before quilting began for the day, and at the end of the day that same daughter cleaned the floor again, picking up small threads and putting away needles. Mrs. Opio's son, George Mundon, would sometimes help by relaxing the tension on the quilt when his mother's stitching came too close to the wood frame, so that she could keep her quilting lines even.

Whatever money Mrs. Opio earned for quilting was put toward the education of her children, but most of her quilts were given to family and friends.

Among the other Hawaiian quilts in the collection at Grove Farm was one made by Emily

Lahapa Kamakalii Opiopio Mundon Opio
c. 1930

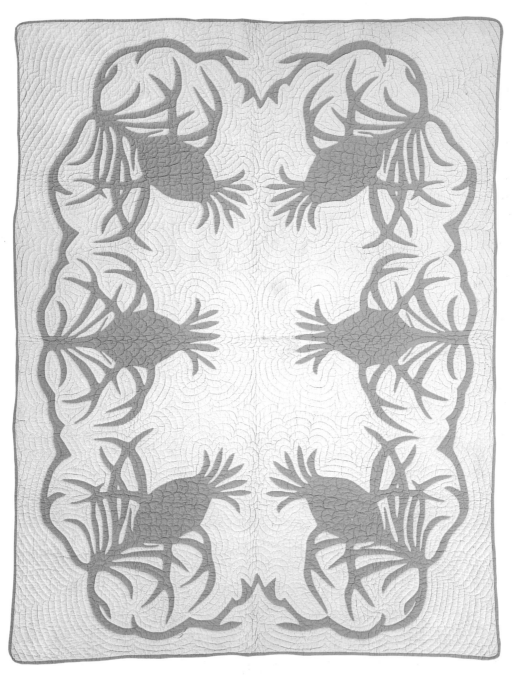

Hala Kahiki
Pineapple
78 x 60 inches. c. 1940. Made by Mrs. Lahapa Kamakalii Opiopio Mundon Opio.
This quilt belonged to Elsie Wilcox.

Salai I Makanani who was born in 1904 at Hanalei, Kauai and later moved with her family to Nawiliwili. She was seventeen when she decided she wanted to learn to quilt. Rather than learning directly from her mother, Emilia I, it was decided that she would go to Kalihiwai and apprentice with Mrs. Apaka, the late Alfred Apaka's mother. Mrs. I and Emily felt that she would learn different techniques or stitches which they could use in their quilting. There was a bit of difficulty though, because Mrs. Apaka was right-handed while Emily was left-handed — as was her mother.

Emily I married John Makanani in 1922 and they had five sons. She and her mother quilted together in the parlor of the family home at Nawiliwili for about ten years, making fifteen Hawaiian quilts. Each felt it helped to have the other one there, giving encouragement to keep working on a quilt.

Many Hawaiian mothers felt they should make a quilt for each of their children as a remembrance and for that reason Emily gave a quilt to each of her sons. She stopped quilting in 1930 when her third son was born. According to Emily's brother, Gabriel I, sources for patterns came from their mother. *"My mother was gifted with dreams in which she would have ideas for quilt patterns. The next morning she would describe the pattern to Emily, who sketched the idea and cut it out."*

Emily Salai I Makanani
c. 1950

Pika Pua Lilia
Vase of Lilies
76 x 74 inches. 1952. Made by Mrs. Emily Salai I Makanani.
"This quilt was bought from Emily Makanani in February, 1952. It has always been kept at the Grove Farm house." EHW notes.

Pua Nana La or Pua o Ka La
Sunflower
87 x 86 inches. c. 1940. Made by Mrs. Moki of Hanapepe.
"This quilt was bought by Elsie Wilcox in July of 1940, and has been kept at the Grove Farm house. A purple sun-flower quilt was given to Sarah Langston of Mississippi in 1939." EHW notes.

Peahi o Kaiulani
Kaiulani's Fan
85 x 86 inches. Date unknown. Quilter unknown.
"This quilt was bought in 1941 from a man who came to the door at Grove Farm. Mrs. Lydia Waiau gave the name and says it is an old pattern. Her mother had a quilt something like this pattern. Also, her husband's family had one." EHW notes.

Kukaua

Kukaua was the name given to a mountain house built by Hans Isenberg on the rim of Kilohana crater above Lihue. Hans' older brother Paul wrote to him from Bremen, Germany in 1899: "*. . .I am glad that your mountain house is finished at Kukaua . . .*"

Kukaua Mountain House on Kilohana Crater rim c. 1905

The Wilcox Quilts in Hawaii

Ethel Damon wrote of Paul Isenberg's visit to Molokoa, his brother's home outside Lihue,

. . . From this cottage veranda at Molokoa one could see, on the edge of Kilohana crater, an hour's easy horseback ride mauka beyond German Forest, the new Kukaua house which had just been finished. And during his first visit in 1900, days of unmixed joy were spent at this mountain house, where one could take in at a single revolving glance the whole green valley of Lihue, backed with the blue of mountain range and faced with an edge of black rock and white surf, reaching into the limitless blue of the North Pacific. There on the lanai Paul Isenberg often sat, looking from the fields of Kipu and Haiku on the south, across over the mill and the fair, green acres of Lihue itself, past the second mill and broad fields of Hanamaulu to the eastward, where the low Kalepa Ridge throws out its protecting arm along the seacoast toward the deep cut of the Wailua River Valley, which narrows and divides into two winding branches as it nears the north where great mountains stand perpetual guard . . .

After many years' use, the Isenbergs left their Kukaua property to their family sugar company, Lihue Plantation. In 1946 Grove Farm Company leased Kukaua from Lihue Plantation for use by the Wilcox family and company employees as a mountain retreat. Miss Elsie and Miss Mabel enjoyed using the house and brought two of their Hawaiian quilts, *Poinsettia* and *Lilia,* for the beds there. The unquilted *Pikake* became the tablecloth for the large round table in the main room. All three quilt patterns stood out against the dark-stained interiors of the old mountain house, where a carved wooden bear stood guard over the staircase to the second floor.

Grove Farm Company gave up its lease of Kukaua in 1970, and Miss Mabel arranged for the return of her furnishings. Kukaua was demolished six years later.

Kihapai Pua o Kauai
Garden Island
83 x 69 inches. Date unknown. Made by Mrs. Lydia Ellis Waiau.
"The original '*Kihapai Pua o Kauai*' was designed by Mrs. Kaneakua, made by Mrs. Kalei Montgomery and was owned by Mrs.
Dora Isenberg. This copy from the original pattern was made by Mrs. Lydia Waiau for Elsie Wilcox." EHW notes.

Poinsettia
82 x 80 inches. Pre-1933. Made by Mrs. Lydia Ellis Waiau.
This quilt belonged to Elsie Wilcox. It was included in the Mokihana Club Exhibit, taken to Kukaua in 1946,
and is now kept at Grove Farm.

Pikake
94 x 89 inches. c. 1940. Unquilted. Appliquer unknown.
"This unquilted quilt pattern was bought from Mrs. Kitkowsky of Koloa by Mabel Wilcox in 1940. It was hemmed for a tablecloth and taken to Kukaua in 1946, and is now kept at Grove Farm." EHW notes.

Lilia
Water Lily
82 x 74 inches. Date unknown. Quilter unknown.
"This quilt was made by an old lady in Kapaa who was a relative of Mrs. Kamanuwai. It was bought by Elsie Wilcox and was taken to Kukaua in 1946. It is now kept at the Grove Farm house." EHW notes.

Ethel Damon's Collection

Ethel Mosley Damon
c. 1900

S even quilts were added to the Wilcox collection by longtime friend Ethel Mosley Damon. She was born in Honolulu in 1883, the daughter of Edward Chenery and Cornelia Beckwith Damon and was educated at Punahou and Wellesley College.

In 1917 she sailed with Mabel Wilcox to LeHavre, France to work with the First World War effort. Miss Damon acted as secretary and translator to Dr. E. A. Park of the American Red Cross. Together with Miss Mabel she was decorated with the Order of Elizabeth from the Queen of the Belgians and the bronze medal of the City of LeHavre.

Miss Damon returned to Hawaii where she began a career of writing history. Her publications span all the islands and many of their families and churches. She was a frequent visitor to Grove Farm and part of the family life. She was fascinated with the history of the islands and would sit with George, Sam, Emma, Elsie and Mabel Wilcox in an evening, drawing out wonderful stories of the Waioli childhood of 'the old gentlemen'. She acted as scribe to G. N. Wilcox's stories of his varied business ventures. As she was always certain to record their expressions or reactions to their own stories, her notes have contributed richly to this and other publications about the Wilcoxes.

Another interest of Miss Damon's was landscaping and flower arranging. She was actively involved in the landscaping of Grove Farm, Waioli, G. N. Wilcox Memorial Hospital, Lihue Union Church, and the Mission Houses in Honolulu. While she would travel to gather information for her books, she always returned to Grove Farm where she died in 1965.

Hoeha Puuwai
Heartache or Pain
83 x 81 inches. Date unknown. Made by Alice Kaliokuoluna.
This quilt was part of the Ethel Damon collection.

Name Unknown
80 x 78½ inches. Date unknown. Quilter unknown.
This quilt is part of the Ethel Damon collection.

Coat-of-Arms and Hibiscus
93 x 74 inches. Embroidered. Date unknown. Quilter unknown.
This quilt was originally square with red trim around all four sides, but later a piece of mattress padding
was added to lengthen it and create two rounded corners. One of Ethel Damon's quilts.

Hawaiian Flag and Coat-of-Arms
86 x 84 inches. Date unknown. Quilter unknown.
This quilt from the Ethel Damon collection is made with red, white and blue cotton fabric while the yellow is of satin material.

Hawaiian Flag and Coat-of-Arms
Detail

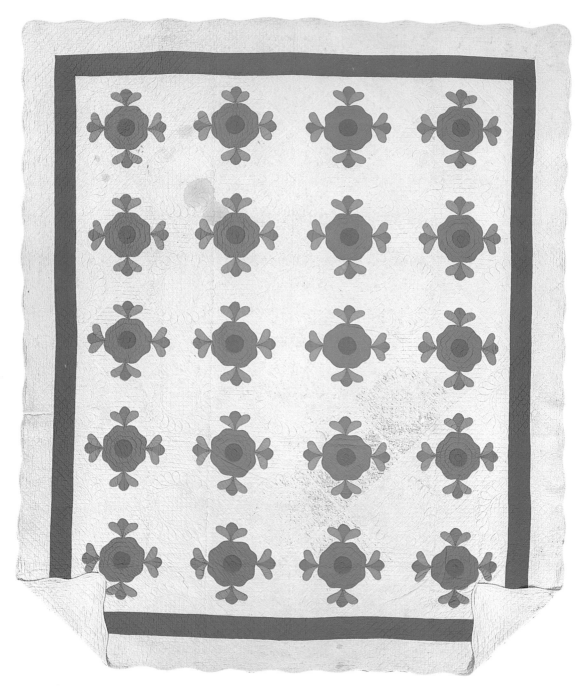

American Appliqued Quilt
91 x 77 inches. Date unknown. Quilter unknown.
This quilt is from the Ethel Damon collection.

American Appliqued Flowers
95 x 72 inches. Date unknown. Quilter unknown.
This quilt is part of the Ethel Damon collection.

Name Unknown
87½ x 82¼ inches. Date unknown. Quilter unknown.
This unquilted coverlet is one of Ethel Damon's collection.

The 1983 Exhibition and Grove Farm Today

Mabel Wilcox announced her plans for the present Grove Farm Homestead museum in 1971, and in the following years her staff continued the household and garden routines established by her mother and maintained by her sister and herself through two generations. When she died seven years later it was the first time in more than a century that no member of the Wilcox family lived in the old home.

Miss Mabel had loaned several quilts to exhibits at the Kauai Museum over the years, but the community had never seen the family quilt collection in its entirety. In 1983 Grove Farm Homestead put the collection of quilts on exhibit at the Kauai Museum. The exhibition was originally scheduled for December, 1982. It was designed around a Christmas theme, using the quilts as banners suspended from the second-floor space at Kauai Museum above an old-fashioned island Christmas tree with candles and old decorations. There were also to be exhibited music boxes, dolls, and other antique toys from both the Kauai Museum and Grove Farm Homestead collections.

Preparations began with Rhoda Komuro, a Honolulu textile conservator, inspecting the condition of the quilt collection. She then worked with more than two dozen women from the Kauai Senior Centers Inc., who volunteered many days hand stitching muslin and Velcro strips onto the Hawaiian quilts so that they would be properly displayed at the exhibition. The second floor of the Grove Farm house was transformed into a tranquil sewing bee where the women sat on sheets on the floor with quilts spread out before them.

At the same time wooden frames were being constructed for the exhibit design and oral history interviews were taking place with many family members of the known quilters, who described designs, techniques and family life. Exhibition invitations were printed, based on early Christmas cards in the Grove Farm collection, and were carried to the Lihue Post Office through a heavy wind on November 23, 1982. The wind turned into Hurricane Iwa which resulted in roof damage to the Kauai Museum and a three-month delay in the exhibition.

The Wilcox Quilts in Hawaii

On March 9, 1983, the Wilcox Hawaiian quilt collection was presented to the island community. Thirty-six quilts lined the walls of the two-story main gallery of the Kauai Museum. Biographies of five quilters were proudly shared by their children, bringing the histories of many of the quilts alive. The Makanani, Montgomery, Opio, Waiau, and Waiuli family members, who had shared their reminiscences, clustered by the creations of their mothers or aunties, greeting friends while Hawaiian music filled the exhibit space.

Julie Yukimura and Irmalee Pomroy arranged for expert island quilters to give lectures on the history of quilting and weekend workshops for timid novices. One workshop was not only taught by a known quilter, but also included help from her husband, daughter and son-in-law. Throughout the exhibition an unquilted piece was set up on a quilting frame and was quilted by both experienced and beginning quilters. This not only was useful as a training project but allowed visitors to see work in progress and to ask questions of the quilters during the exhibition. By May 31st, close to 5,000 people had seen the collection, many of them taking part in the planned activities over the three-month showing.

The exhibit was taken down and the quilts returned to Grove Farm where the muslin and Velcro strips were removed. After being aired individually for a day on the *koa* railing, the quilts were folded and put back in their storage chests. This traditional annual airing, which proved so successful over the past fifty years, continues to conserve the collection of the Wilcox family's quilts in Hawaii.

The 1983 Wilcox Quilt Exhibit held at the Kauai Museum.